u&i

THIS IS A STORY SPELLED U & I

CASSANDRA SMITH

OMNIDAWN PUBLISHING
OAKLAND, CALIFORNIA
2015

Cover image: Cassandra Smith, *held collage*, 2013.
(polaroid photograph taken in portland, or, 2002;
various found postcards dated aprox. 1901-1914)

Offset printed in the United States
by Edwards Brothers Malloy, Ann Arbor, Michigan
On 55# Heritage Book Cream White Antique
Acid Free Archival Quality Recycled Paper
with Rainbow FSC Certified Colored End Papers

Library of Congress
Cataloging-in-Publication Data

Smith, Cassandra, 1980-
  [Poems. Selections]
  u&i / Cassandra Smith.
     pages cm
  ISBN 978-1-63243-010-6 (pbk. : alk. paper)
  I. Title. II. Title: u & i.
  PS3619.M55455A6 2015
  811'.6--dc23
                              2015017613

Published by Omnidawn Publishing, Oakland, California
www.omnidawn.com   (510) 237-5472   (800) 792-4957
          10 9 8 7 6 5 4 3 2 1
          ISBN: 978-1-63243-010-6

these are the people to thank and to hold closely

soon after the night i married the ghost erika staiti and i were driving in a car in berkeley and then in oakland and she and i got into a fighting match about how Unicorns Are Not Real Cassie. but i didn't mean things that have legs and horns. it is not like this. it is something else.

erika staiti and samantha giles and kate pringle and stan apps and rusty morrison and rebecca stoddard and sara mumolo and truong tran and david buuck and bhanu kapil and laynie browne and selah saterstrom and melissa benham and mathew timmons and mathias svalina and rozzell medina and ross khalsa and art medlar and lara durback and elka weber and julianna leskie and nik de dominic and levi pratt and kathryn stull and sharon zetter and jeffrey schrader and jeffrey melendez and frank brash.

brent cunningham is in one of these poems.
lucas and lucy are in all of them.

also the journals:
the offending adam, *saginaw*, *joyland*, *the medium* via *the volta*, *pilgrimage*, *where eagles dare*, *comma*, *poetry*, *THEthe* via called back books.

this book is staiti's fault.

the last poem is for vu.

U&I IN WORDS

I.
with which memories do you feel most often afraid

II.
except here. u&i began to question the direction of a path
that would lead to unnatural feathers in a very natural spot
in the undergrowth of the forest

III.
u&i didn't often rationalize before a thought was formed

IV.
on the matter of u&i

V.
u&i on the matter of forests

VI.
the dream of a house with two doors

VII.
u&i were not he nor she nor we but something different.
a singular of sincere

VIII.
u&i entwined

XVIII.

u&i as a word of two wons

XIX.

u&i: a gain

XX.

u&i began in a forest and u&i ended in a wood. we would
like to separate ourselves for a moment and tell you a story:

XXI.

the beginning began and init u&i were formed and in
formed, we must tell you a story

XXII.

it is always beginning because it is always celebration

XXIII.

u&i began to plunder as if plunder could become a word
that would mean a stillness of everything else

XXIV.

u&i wrote a book about what it was like to live alone in this
forest

XXV.

u&i began to sink into the whole that sitting in the same
chair would make

XXVI.

u&i kept cards around the house, from places it had once
been important to see

XXVII.
a curious of gentlemen invites u&i from a clearing .

XXVIII.
u&i concedes

XXIX.
u&i moved to a city from a place of how the meadows move

XXX.
u&i from a country had learned to care about where to rest

XXXI.
u&i moved from a city into a room where things could be
heard when nothing seemed to be happening

XXXII.
when u&i went to a place it became a gathering

XXXIII.
u&i sat in the back

XXXIV.
u&i heard a song from where it had once come from

XXXV.
u&i as logic of pronouns

XXXVI.
u&i began as a voice and then u&i became a song

XXXVII.
u&i were unsure

XXXVIII.
u&i found someone to fall in love with

XXXIX.
u&i opened the paper

XL.
u&i drew stories about the meadow lost

XLI.
u&i had a dream of before and before had been made of
numbers that were not a balance of five

XLII.
u&i met another and u&i forgot the forest and u&i
forgot everything

XLIII.
u&i and &other

XLIV.
u&i and &other would try to speak in city voices but we
were not sure of the words and we would stumble and
we would want to be alone again so that we were not so
desperately failing

XLV.
u&i began as a place where there was never an alone

XLVI.

when u&i would have emotions the emotions would only be
made of things that had always ever been known. there was
meadow and forest and wood and when u&i tried to feel
anything else it became frightening the way forests are felt
by those who are not sure how to feel them

XLVII.

u&i gets prophetic and u&i hears what another near will say

XLVIII.

when u&i would listen to something it would have to be
intimate because u&i could not bear to be misconstrued

XLIX.

once u&i met a girl and fell in love

L.

u&i as longing or languid

LI.

u&i on &other and the adventure

LII.

&other would not endure when another near would wander

LIII.

&other would be gone but still there was the rest

LIV.

u&i and a beast

LV.

u&i found wit and wonder and u&i objected to one within
the other but u&i had never been a species of fury

LVI.

u&i with the beast would forget we had just met and when
we learned the parts of becoming a part of the same thing
we would notice the drifting like snow

LVII.

once it was said there is no domestic but once from the
beginning of us came with the risk

LVIII.

i don't really know the name of how my hands weep

LIX.

unicorns are not smart creatures

LX.

once u&i were together

WITH WHICH MEMORIES DO YOU FEEL MOST OFTEN AFRAID?

u&i didn't often feel afraid. this was a constant in the unnatural order of how things are placed. u&i would set a book down to know it wouldn't move until someone meant to read it, or dust beneath. the same with jars and windows and houses. these things did not move unless intentionally and intention in regards to movement was a natural process of the imaginary. this pleased u&i best, the movement of dancing. each foot would be set upon the floor in certain ways one did not know the answer to, and there would always be an organic response that one would attend. sometimes small trees would grow from the wood floors. also this was ordinary and u&i would not worry about the stains of water upon the carpets because carpets could always be taken into the yard and thoroughly washed.

EXCEPT HERE. U&I BEGAN TO QUESTION THE DIRECTION OF
A PATH THAT WOULD LEAD TO UNNATURAL FEATHERS IN A
VERY NATURAL SPOT IN THE UNDERGROWTH OF THE FOREST

there was a knowledge of birds but not of this color, which made

the world of a small place very unfamiliar. it was the uncertainty

of a certain familiar that would cause a trepidation in each step

but the feathers were collected and put into a book and soon then

forgotten.

U&I DIDN'T OFTEN RATIONALIZE BEFORE A THOUGHT WAS FORMED

if, upon an inquiry, there was a general excitement about a subject, u&i would insist upon talking very excitedly about the nothing it seemed to surround. this nothing was always filled to the most incremental of means, but could never be understood if an outsider tried to rationalize. it would often begin as a small plague in the brain for each party, of thoughts that couldn't be re-formed into anything else.

this was thought to suit u&i just fine. a happiness borne from every rounded design.

u&i would often dream of moving to the country, where an abandoned house would be retrieved from a certain shade of the overgrown, and objects that had been collected over the years would be mixed in with objects that had collected over the years and many rusty things would stay where found or be placed where others could not be. it was a complicated dream, this house in a clearing. a clutter would surround each of any moment. u&i would argue sometimes that there was not much difference between moving to find an abandoned house of accumulated matter and moving somewhere that had not been abandoned and where one could find nothing of immediate accumulation. and also not moving at all. u&i did not often feel regret but when this thought would find its way into occurrence there was always a sturdy and lingering gloom.

is it a city or a country or is it only alone. u&i would ask but there was no another near.

ON THE MATTER OF U&I

u&i moved to a wood or u&i stayed somewhere else. this is the only rule.

the myth of walking was never put to any accuracy. as a genuine
when we would stray we were always aware of a certain treading,
a softening of occurring but there are things when one walks
that cannot be undone. as we, we believe this is the beginning of
chivalry: the unicorn of gentlemen.

how one might roam. how two might meander.

THE DREAM OF A HOUSE WITH TWO DOORS

u&i went for a walk and could feel the nettles stinging each finger but there was an impossible placement of pain. there was something to be said of circulation but the curtains behind the windows had each been painted shut.

U&I WERE NOT HE NOR SHE NOR WE BUT SOMETHING
DIFFERENT. A SINGULAR OF SINCERE

u&i would try not to lie about where things began or how they
were invented but the hardest part was figuring the simple logic
of one or two. u&i would like to be one made of two or two into
something very large but sometimes it is very hard to be constantly
convinced. u&i could feel one body against another body and
something would always threaten to fracture.

U&I ENTWINED

u&i always mean to begin but instead are always just beginning. a sadness
in this understood logic.

left as you and i alone,
an isolation.

maybe one&us must find some string or bit of surface.

forgetful, one of u&i embark on an adventure in the cold.
the other tells a story.

THE CASSAMANTHRA PROJECT

it is sad, but we have discovered that we hate unicorns. unicorns are small magical creatures that tread lightly so as not to intrude upon even the ground, and we all think that is fine and (dandy), but also we do not buy it. when we tread, we tread heavily and there are footprints, and then we take out our measurement sticks and we measure these prints, be they in sand or snow, and what we do next is write them down. and the measurements are never unicorns. they are impressions of very big feet in very heavy boots, and tromping is all about everything good anyways, because how else are we to feel that we are having an impact on one dimensional vibrating strings, because the whole notion of one dimensional vibrating strings is really fucking out-there to us, even considering how we have been lying all along and really do love the genuine of unicorns (which is the proper plural of a mostly singular specimen).

U&I

dear then us.

IT HAS LOST ITS STEAD OF CANTERING AND HOW TO
CANTER IS TO RETURN TO WHERE WE WERE NOT (SMALL,
DIRT ROAD) WELCOME

or recounting of methods(say) madness was lost &

oh deer with what subtle

i aint or iaint

or i aint quite sure where

there is a u&i to continue

DEAR U OR I,

i seem to cant go on without you.

.

I'VE GOT THIS IDEA, YOU SEE, AND THEN WITH FRIGHT AND
WHAT FOLLOWS

U&I HAVE FOUND THE PATTERN AND U&I BEGIN TO BELIEVE
IN LONESOME

or shaky through leaves

and sullen

U&I: A PART

u&i began an inner monologue of what might happen were one divided multilaterally. this made u&i laugh, what sound a multilatter might make. but then with how broken (destroying)the sound must be.

somehow it suddenly became strange, an awkward of occurrence,
how one thing could be better than anything else. how might you
or i know the difference between this, which is good, and that,
which is so much better. this and that were never before an amount
of comparison. looking at the world through suddenly what is best
became very lonely, as this best might never be seen by anyone else:
a question of this best is best because no one is near to dispute. but
would that my dueling skills were defined.

ONCE A MATTER OF FIGHTING WAS INVENTED, BUT ONCE WE
FORGOT HOW TO PROCEED

u&i sat so closely there was no turning towards anything else. in a

box or in a room or in an anywhere, u&i focused until once again

the differences became a sound of the untensing of reason. it was

best this way, u&i decided, laughing because this best would always

win.

riddle:

a curious of gentlemen and a genuine of unicorn meet in a wood.

u&i couldn't stop laughing.

U&I: A GAIN

you and i would sit and laugh and laugh and laugh.

U&I BEGAN IN A FOREST AND U&I ENDED IN A WOOD.
WE WOULD LIKE TO SEPARATE OURSELVES FOR A MOMENT
AND TELL YOU A STORY:

u&i began in a forest or u&i ended in a wood. we would sit together

and find the best of things and hold them closely. this holding

& closely took an entire lifetime so we conspired together to

change a natural occurrence of ending and death and, being as

how we started as two-and-not-one, we took that second part

of our lifetimes and in our forest and in our wood we held this

very closely. our act of living still while also again didn't bother

us because in this part of the story, only we knew that there

was an us to distinguish.

THE BEGINNING BEGAN AND INIT U&I WERE FORMED AND IN
FORMED, WE MUST TELL YOU A STORY

it was snowing and i went for a walk. it kept snowing and i could
find nothing between where it was snowing and where, someplace
else, it wasn't. i grew very afraid. a snowglobe but you were outside
the silent plastic walls. i began to jump and through jumping leapt
the whole thing off of your desk and in falling you picked me up
and we never again stepped foot inside a building of where things
are done.

IT IS ALWAYS BEGINNING BECAUSE IT IS ALWAYS CELEBRATION

u&i found a photograph of looking at a place through a small hole
and we never left the room we made of it.

U&I BEGAN TO PLUNDER AS IF PLUNDER COULD BECOME A WORD
THAT WOULD MEAN A STILLNESS OF EVERYTHING ELSE

u&i as silhouette of laughing and dancing.

u&i in footsteps.

u&i in falling in a garden.

u&i as an object of interruption, a sound but what in this case may be

following through.

are we an obsession or a device. are we a we if there is no difference

between.

U&I WROTE A BOOK ABOUT WHAT IT WAS LIKE TO LIVE ALONE IN
THIS FOREST

there was one chair and one desk and u&i would struggle with where one should rest.

there was a bed on the floor, a bed on the forest.

u&i had wanted to curl into all these places of only one thing.

one holding.

one speaking.

one of only one anything.

words were hard to come by some days, and u&i holding this only could find

nothing of another near.

U&I BEGAN TO SINK INTO THE WHOLE THAT SITTING IN THE SAME CHAIR WOULD MAKE

it was hard to leave what had been formed, and what had been formed around.

u&i in this forest in this chair in this place of what only u&i saw and could saw into smaller pieces would take these pieces and try to piece them together.

U&I KEPT CARDS AROUND THE HOUSE, FROM PLACES IT HAD
ONCE BEEN IMPORTANT TO SEE

u&i alone in a forest were the only subject of all of these cards,

alone on a wall in a forest. these cards were a stack on a bookshelf,

a stack on the floor. a stranger would enter and the cards would tell

stories of how to tell more.

A CURIOUS OF GENTLEMEN INVITES U&I FROM A CLEARING

u&i wondered what it would be like to put on a gentleman suit and hold things once they had been taken. a joy of having something that could be held anew.

u&i could not be sure what to do with the things of someone else, the things that were once held in a different other hands. each thing had a hesitance of having what does not belong.

u&i planned a parade for the worry of things taken, for how to hold and how to continue with holding. u&i would leave and u&i would walk to where the holdings could be returned.

U&I CONCEDES

entering a city became a humor of taking, or where to be placed.
u&i couldn't help but continue.

entering a city was made of a measurement into how many things
could be placed beneath the things that are left behind. how to
carry and to carry over. things should be brought and things that
were not should be bought and everything should fit until it spills
over and then a bargain should be made. there are rules for too
much. there are rules for not enough. there are things to learn
about how to enter a city and how to proceed.

u&i stood closely.
entering a city became a bile.

U&I MOVED TO A CITY FROM A PLACE OF HOW THE MEADOWS
MOVE

there are only five things that any one person in conversation with
another person cares about. this is the first rule of a city: you
cannot have more. in a meadow there are places to put everything
because everything is only made of these places to put them. in a
city a person in conversation will build things for the places they
are putting places into, they will hold things until another person
in conversation notices and also begins to want to put these places
into other places.

u&i had not always been myth of animal,
of other recognizably agreeing.

u&i had been other things before.

it needed to be loved at an angle. it needed to be framed. it needed
to have so many things around it so that contexts could be made
and re-formed and then it needed to be moved in case someone
was offended. it needed to be held and then for a stranger to say harsh
things to it, in order for it to wonder if it had been wrong all along.
it sat in a stillness worse than discarded.

u&i couldn't do this anymore.

u&i invented an address.

U&I MOVED FROM A CITY INTO A ROOM WHERE THINGS COULD
BE HEARD WHEN NOTHING SEEMED TO BE HAPPENING

there would be attention to how to slice a food in the proper measure for eating.

there would be rules for how to open, how to close, how to follow and to lock behind.

there would be lists of things to see, things one should have known.

there would be this or that.

this or that would continue each time again more pronounced than
before. this would be large. this would have loom. this would be
indistinguishable from any other this and what was once a game of pieces
became the only thing to do:

i found this for you.

WHEN U&I WENT TO A PLACE IT BECAME A GATHERING

u&i had never been to a place before and the things that had gathered were around us and everything was made of words and how to make more words and how these words would grow into things that might become large. u&i made words to fit with the things and to fit with how the things gather and u&i learned something new and u&i forgot everything else. there is nothing else because there is gather and u&i cried.

in the back there is stillness and in the back there is how does this work. in a city everything is how does this work and how things work is made of matter which is very important. all of our meadow had been planted into this yard and we couldn't go near. our meadow was planted and tended and the things of matter would walk into it and dig their heels. this meadow is so lovely. this meadow makes me feel like i shouldn't wear shoes. don't you love this meadow and u&i would want to put their shoes back onto their feet and tell them to leave the meadow very alone.

u&i remembered how sad things had been in the forest. how things were only one or only two or only what it was like to hold something closely and for something to not be there. u&i had been lost and a small another was placed in a branch, for u&i to find later. u&i laughed like this was a bird and u&i packed this away for when it was needed. u&i held it in this city because it was a branch that hadn't been taken or made into something or ever harshly spoken to. this branch was the something that wasn't there and u&i wanted to go home so badly.

harshly is the only how to live in a city u&i could say.

u&i would be we when we were with others and u&i would be i
when u&i were alone and u&i would be you when u&i were speaking
to each other and u&i would worry that every concurrence might
become felled.

there is always a place in a room. this is the place of hiding and this is the place where nothing can be found even if someone is looking. this is the place where u&i planted a meadow and no one in a city could find it. u&i had become so sad that this was now the place of where the meadow grew. u&i wanted to invite someone into this meadow, into this place of where nothing could be found, but u&i would say all of the wrong words to the someones in the city. u&i knew a place could be gilded, but u&i had only started to know the loyalty of alone.

u&i did not know the best way to break apart and come together and tell each other about what apart was like and how apart was now made of everything else. this was the story: u&i were one and then u&i quarreled and u&i left each other and when u&i were together again u&i quarreled with everything else.

this is a simple story.

U&I FOUND SOMEONE TO FALL IN LOVE WITH

u&i did not know how to do this but u&i were trying so hard. u&i listened to the saddest songs. u&i and another would walk to places and everywhere were hands holding other hands they could not see.

there was a forest on fire and there was a forest that had been the forest of u&i and this was suddenly no longer a place to return. u&i sat in a small corner of meadow in a city of bricks and wept because now there was nowhere else.

our every else had been ruined while u&i were away.

U&I DREW STORIES ABOUT THE MEADOW LOST

u&i worried that our bodies were growing differently. u&i clung to each other and after the fire it became very important that we were two who were clinging. there was at least another when there was nothing else and we remembered when we had fallen in love with something far away. we could play this on repeat because in a city there is always something new to buy and we could walk to where we would buy them. we bought the same recordings and the same things to play them on and we kept buying these things because we could not stand to see our empty hands. we could not stand to hold them.

U&I HAD A DREAM OF BEFORE AND BEFORE HAD BEEN MADE
OF NUMBERS THAT WERE NOT A BALANCE OF FIVE

there is a secret balance of five in making a meadow. now that our
meadow was gone it became important to explain this in diagram
for others to make and to follow. the balance of five is a story of
hiding and growing and the after. the balance of five is a moth and
the wings. u&i did not like to admit that there were other important
creatures because we were a unison and we would sing so loud in
the clearing. the balance of five was made of a large beginning and a
small between. there would be a middle that would mirror and the
end would end in an opposite decline. u&i hated that we had been
blamed for moths but we had loved them so gently.

U&I MET ANOTHER AND U&I FORGOT THE FOREST AND U&I FORGOT EVERYTHING

it was easy, this other. there was an other and there was something new and there was no remembering a forest that was no longer there. there were small sprouts growing where once were trees but even the sprouts were far away. u&i hadn't considered that an other might be hiding from the same forest. u&i had never seen an other there before.

in the forest there is one tree or three trees or one root or this shadow and things are not unknown because there has never been anything else. u&i with this other did not understand what was left to count or that there should be counting or how to count without stopping and u&i could feel the uncertainty like nettles. they would sting and they would enter and what should have made for an easing of pain would lodge in our fingers and every time we would touch it it would numb a new part of our parts that were starting to disappear.

U&I AND &OTHER WOULD TRY TO SPEAK IN CITY VOICES
BUT WE WERE NOT SURE OF THE WORDS AND WE WOULD
STUMBLE AND WE WOULD WANT TO BE ALONE AGAIN SO
THAT WE WERE NOT SO DESPERATELY FAILING

and the&other

ohother.

ohbrotherohbother

ohcanter

ohreturn

U&I BEGAN AS A PLACE WHERE THERE WAS NEVER AN ALONE

an alone is made of where things aren't and u&i in the middle of meadow and forest and wood had never been alone because nothing had ever been taken. in forest and meadow and wood there were only things to look at and things to hold. there was the smallest light to play in and this was the place of holding another closely. worry was a thing to be done only to the things that would enter and when they would enter they would soon prepare to leave.

WHEN U&I WOULD HAVE EMOTIONS THE EMOTIONS WOULD ONLY BE MADE OF THINGS THAT HAD ALWAYS EVER BEEN KNOWN. THERE WAS MEADOW AND FOREST AND WOOD AND WHEN U&I TRIED TO FEEL ANYTHING ELSE IT BECAME FRIGHTENING THE WAY FORESTS ARE FELT BY THOSE WHO ARE NOT SURE HOW TO FEEL THEM

u&i when the forest was gone would want to apologize for being so scared. so scared of things that weren't there and scared of the pace and scared of the lack and scared of what other things u&i would have to be to see the things that were important now that there was nothing else. nothing was very important to everyone in a city and u&i could not see the nothing and u&i could not touch it and u&i would pretend we were looking at it but what it was became a place of away. u&i would find away in the nothing everyone was looking at and when everyone began to look towards u&i we became very away.

U&I GETS PROPHETIC AND U&I HEARS WHAT ANOTHER NEAR
WILL SAY

(hello.)

hello is all they always ever say and u&i would say aloud the most
intricate bits of a forest and there had been understanding here
and there had been holding so closely. hello would echo and hello
would exclude and hello was pulling and it was near. hello would
only ever mean that there was distance and there was intention
implying this distance because hello meant you had not been there
before. even when u&i would say nothing there was knowledge and
there was growing and u&i would sing a distant softest embrace.
u&i would never dare say hello to things when we meant it.

WHEN U&I WOULD LISTEN TO SOMETHING IT WOULD HAVE
TO BE INTIMATE BECAUSE U&I COULD NOT BEAR TO BE
MISCONSTRUED

ONCE U&I MET A GIRL AND FELL IN LOVE

this is what u&i did best, finding a girl in a meadow.

u&i and the girl always would have the same name when we met
and we would look at each other through this name until the girl
in the meadow would hear her name called clearly from another
horizon. the girl would return to her cottage and u&i would be left
to puzzle this loudly. there had been suddenly something and now
there wasn't and this was very new because our forest was hard to
find. every time we would be tricked so synonymously.

u&i would wake and u&i would continue with waking and when u&i began to wake longer into the mornings it was nearly always due to the distance of another. distance is a very hard thing for u&i to understand as distance implies that something else exists. u&i would invent these things to exist and then others to catch and even more to follow but invented matter is a tricky thing to believe in. u&i had hands and shoulders that would fall apart as soon as something near was grasped.

u&i invented another and u&i held this other in the smallest giving hands when u&i encountered something new. the other and &other would look through their invented glass pieces and there soon was no seeing the distinction. the other was made to catch light from the meadow that u&i hid in and it was too tempting to see &other without it.

&OTHER WOULD NOT ENDURE WHEN ANOTHER NEAR
WOULD WANDER

the other was made of how to see and how to see into and how to
see nothing else and when &other began to struggle against this
other &other was no longer sure of the closest place to rest. u&i
could not tell if it was a game of lead or follow or through but
when &other stopped moving u&i mourned so resoundingly.

&OTHER WOULD BE GONE BUT STILL THERE WAS THE REST

u&i would grasp the another and take this into our arms and into windows and houses and this other would be the things of jars and shelves and ceilings and u&i had forgotten we had left the city or that there had been a city or that a city was something outside of the plastic glass walls. u&i would keep the another and the another would wait for a new &other to return.

there is a softness of beasts when they are sleeping and they are sleeping beside the body of a nearer u&i. the beasts of the forest were not an eating beasts nor a chasing beasts but they would rumble below the canopy and u&i learned to tend through what their largest feet would unearth.

U&I FOUND WIT AND WONDER AND U&I OBJECTED TO ONE
WITHIN THE OTHER BUT U&I HAD NEVER BEEN A SPECIES OF
FURY

u&i would listen to how the sound of what a beast could sound
would lumber out of its tongue and then how this would turn to
nag. the uncertainty of whether these beast-things were a thing
that maybe u&i could not endure because u&i were missing some
beast pieces was wondered but u&i had never had the proper bits
to begin.

U&I WITH THE BEAST WOULD FORGET WE HAD JUST MET AND
WHEN WE LEARNED THE PARTS OF BECOMING A PART OF THE
SAME THING WE WOULD NOTICE THE DRIFTING LIKE SNOW

there was not often weather in the meadow but u&i could tell a

changing of seasons by the sound of how the boughs would fail.

winter was a tremble of luster, of nearly gotten. u&i would place

names on the things that had fallen and the names would sting

when they would never be spoken aloud. winter would keep the

names frozen and when it grew colic winter would rid the limbs.

ONCE IT WAS SAID THERE IS NO DOMESTIC BUT ONCE FROM
THE BEGINNING OF US CAME WITH THE RISK

everything is so fucking gilt.

it became again strange, this awkward of paws, how one thing could be drawn to another. there would be a sketch of embrace and then would be the withdrawal. the things held in the most intentional of hands would be chewed and then they would no longer exist. they would become the half things of hollow, the things of no longer glory. i had wanted to hold you and keep holding. i didn't care.

UNICORNS ARE NOT SMART CREATURES

they think this is all there is.

ONCE U&I WERE TOGETHER

u&i were you and i and there was a softness when we spoke. i would say something and you would say something in return. there was no meadow and there was no forest and there were no unicorns because when we spoke it would be directly and we would not have to pretend. you would hold my hand. we would drive in a car. you would tell me i need to get my shit together and we would laugh and i would listen.

Cassandra Smith is a poet and visual artist. She has exhibited her book and photography installations in Oakland, San Francisco, Sacramento, Portland, Chicago, and Memphis. Various writings and poetries have appeared in *The Offending Adam*, *comma, poetry*, *Saginaw*, *Joyland*, *The Medium* via *The Volta*, *Pilgrimage*, *Glitterpony*, *With+Stand*, and others. You can visit her web site at www. moloprojects.org.

u&i
by Cassandra Smith

Cover text set in Perpetua Std.
Interior text set in Perpetua Std, Trajan Pro & Arno Pro.

Cover image: Cassandra Smith, *held collage*, 2013.
(polaroid photograph taken in portland, or, 2002;
various found postcards dated aprox. 1901-1914)

Offset printed in the United States
by Edwards Brothers Malloy, Ann Arbor, Michigan
On 55# Heritage Book Cream White Antique
Acid Free Archival Quality Recycled Paper
with Rainbow FSC Certified Colored End Papers

Publication of this book was made possible in part by gifts from:
Robin & Curt Caton
Deborah Klang Smith
John Gravendyk
Barbara White, Trustee, Leaves of Grass Fund

Omnidawn Publishing
Oakland, California
2015

Rusty Morrison & Ken Keegan, senior editors & co-publishers
Gillian Olivia Blythe Hamel, managing editor
Cassandra Smith, poetry editor & book designer
Peter Burghardt, poetry editor & book designer
Melissa Burke, poetry editor & marketing manager
Sharon Zetter, poetry editor, book designer, & grant writer
Liza Flum, poetry editor
RJ Ingram, poetry editor
Juliana Paslay, fiction editor
Gail Aronson, fiction editor
Josie Gallup, publicity assistant
Sheila Sumner, publicity assistant
Kevin Peters, warehouse manager
Janelle Bonifacio, office assistant
Abbigail Baldys, administrative assistant